Freelance Indoor Snow Globe Shaker:

Bring the enchantment of snow indoors by shaking virtual snow globes for clients.

Remote Ice Cream Flavor Tester:
Taste-test exotic ice cream flavors from the comfort of your couch and share your reviews.

Official Sick Day Generator:

Generate creative and absurd excuses for office workers with your call in sick generating prowess.

Remote Personal Bubble Blower:
Provide virtual bubble-blowing sessions to add a touch of whimsy to people's lives.

Freelance Sock Puppeteer:
Bring sock puppets to life in virtual puppet shows, showcasing your dramatic skills.

Professional Cloud Sitter:
Spend your days gazing at the sky and making sure the clouds are fluffy.

Telepathic Cat Translator:
Offer your services to interpret the mysterious thoughts of feline companions.

Virtual Chill Ambassador:
Promote and celebrate the art of chilling with flair and finesse.

Virtual Marshmallow Roaster:
Share your expertise in the art of roasting virtual marshmallows for a cozy experience.

Chief Daydream Strategist:
Develop strategic daydreaming plans for individuals seeking mental adventures.

Remote Hug Specialist:
Offer virtual hugs to those in need of a comforting embrace.

Expert in Imaginary Friend Conversations:

Offer a hotline for adults seeking imaginary friend conversations.

Chief Procrastination Officer:
Head an organization dedicated to embracing and celebrating procrastination.

Freelance Blanket Fort Architect:
Design and build personalized blanket forts for clients of all ages.

Official Snuggler for Stuffed Animals:

Ensure stuffed animals receive ample snuggling for optimal comfort.

Virtual High-Five Instructor:
Teach the subtle art of the virtual high-five for remote celebrations.

Inventor of the Reverse Alarm Clock:

A clock that helps people maximize their sleep by counting backwards from their wake-up time.

Official Bubble Wrap Popper:
Offer a therapeutic bubble wrap popping service via video calls.

Freelance Pillow Talk Consultant:

Provide engaging and entertaining conversation topics for pillow talk sessions.

Virtual Daydream Architect:
Design, advise and construct customized daydreams.

Remote Cartoon Character Impersonator:
Mimic beloved cartoon characters for personalized video greetings.

Couch Detective:
Solve the mystery of how the house can actually get cleaned from the couch.

Influencer for Introverts:

Share your introverted lifestyle with the world, one cozy post at a time.

Chief Blanket Burrito Maker:
Specialize in the art of creating the perfect blanket cocoon.

Kids Slumber Party Stylist:
Provide personalized recommendations for the perfect pajama ensemble.

Official Procrastination Olympics Judge:

Score and critique your own personal procrastination techniques.

Bedtime Story Inventor:
Create and narrate bedtime stories for adults, to help them sleep better.. or not.

Virtual Sigh Recording Artist:
Offer a collection of personalized sighs for those in need of audible expressions.

Official Cloud Gazer:
Share your cloud-gazing expertise with the world, identifying shapes and patterns.

Remote Fortune Cookie Writer:
Craft humorous, ludicrous and absurd fortunes for fortune cookies.

Meme Historian:
Provide historical context and explanations for classic and modern memes.

MODERN MEME VS CLASSIC MEME

Personal Space Consultant:
Advise people on the optimal arrangement of their personal space for maximum comfort.

Freelance Procrastinator:

Assist others in putting off tasks, offering masterful procrastination techniques.

Avoiding Chores 101

Virtual Stand-Up Philosopher:
Share comedic insights and philosophical musings from the comfort of your bed.

Question the cosmos or the meaning of life?
Debate this over TACO'S!

Virtual Plant Whisperer:
Assist houseplants in reaching their full potential through telepathic communication.

Professional Lullaby Singer:
Sing soothing lullabies to people with a REAL job to help themrelax and unwind.

Expert in Creative Excuses:
Offer personalized and creative excuses for any situation.

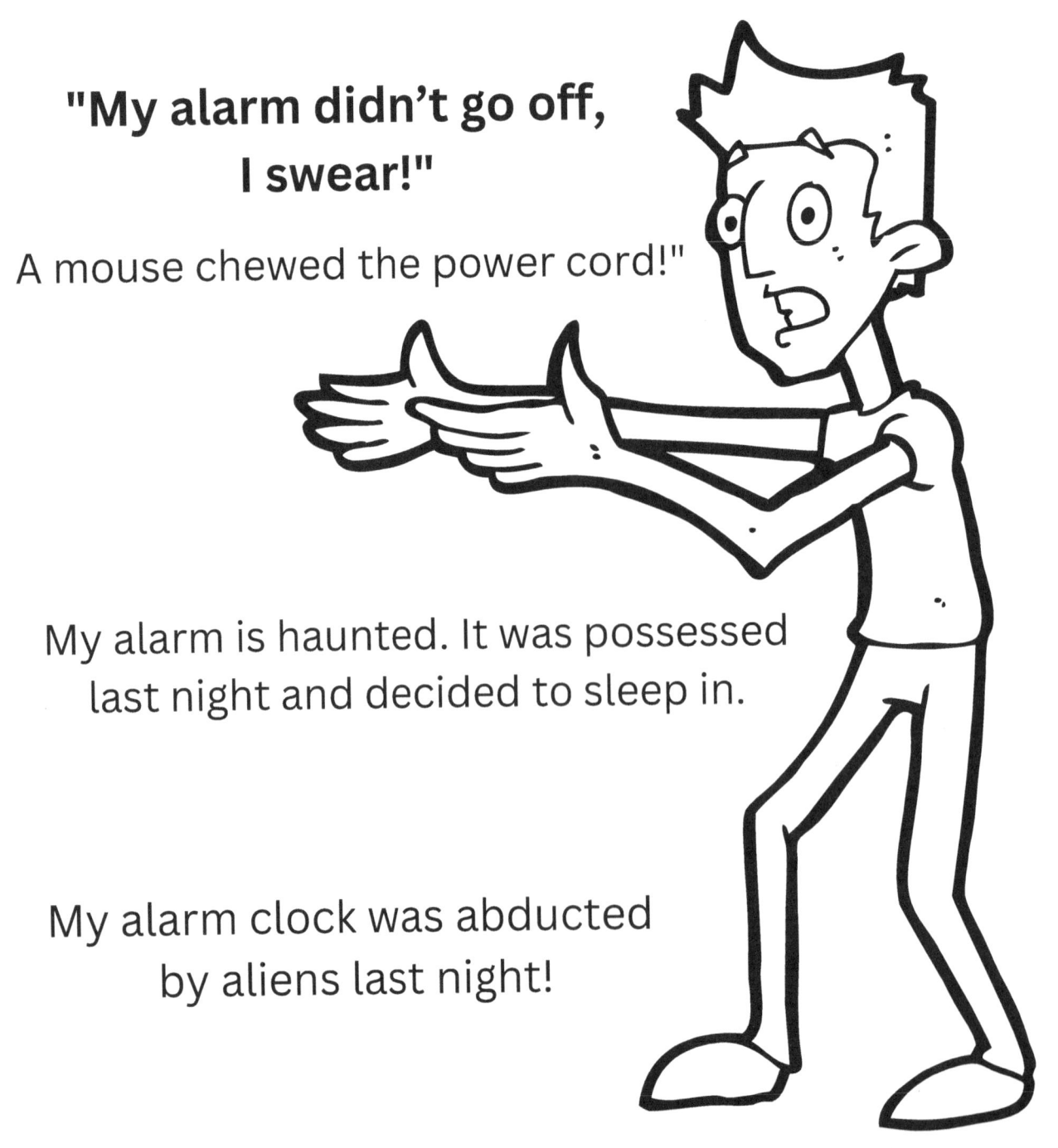

Professional TikTok Viewer

Showcase your unique swiping moves without leaving your living room.

Couch Potato Coach:
Motivate fellow couch potatoes to achieve new levels of laziness.

Remote Tea Taster:
Expertly taste-testvarious teas without leaving your cozy space.

Official Pillow Fluffer:
Provide on-site pillow fluffing services for those in need of extra comfort.

Social Media Sloth:
Document your daily life as the ultimate sloth on social media platforms.

Lazy Life Coach:
Encourage people to embrace the beauty of doing nothing with pride.

Professional TikTok Dancer in Slippers:
Showcase your unique dance moves without leaving your living room.

Ambassador of Pajama Fashion:
Advocate for the latest trends in sleepwear, one lazy outfit at a time.

Remote TV Show Critic:
Offer hilarious commentaries on TV shows and movies from the comfort of your couch.

Pet Psychic for Lazy Cats:
Offer fortune-telling services exclusively for cats who prefer lounging around.

Unicorn Whisperer:
Claim to communicate with mythical creatures and offer consulting services.

Professional Nap Tester:
Get paid to evaluate the comfort of various mattresses and pillows through extensive nap sessions.

Emoji Translator:
Translate messages into emoji form for those who struggle with the written word.

The Lazy Entrepreneur

A Coloring Book For Couch Commanders